IRELAND

HISTORY AND LANDSCAPE

IRELAND

HISTORY AND LANDSCAPE

BRIAN SOLOMON

COMPENDIUM

To the Collins family, my friends in Ireland for more than a decade.

This 2009 edition published by

COMPENDIUM

Project Manager: Peran Publishing
Designer: Ian Hughes
Color Reproduction:
Anorax Imaging Ltd

ISBN-13: 978-1-906347-53-6

Printed and bound in China

PAGE 1: Clinging to the cliff-side above the North Atlantic, Antrim's Dunluce Castle straddles a picturesque promontory which has contributed to the ruin's fame.

PAGES 2–3: Sunset on Coulagh Bay near Gortgariff, Co. Cork on the Beara Peninsula.

RIGHT: The basalt columns of the Giant's Causeway. *Richard Cummins/Corbis*

CONTENTS

ACKNOWLEDGMENTS

In the last ten years, I have enjoyed many trips exploring Ireland's towns and countryside–traveling both alone and with friends, and I have made friends along the way. I've spent many hours, camera in hand, photographing and perusing Irish literature, and visiting people. I've met many people who have helped me in innumerable ways. They have suggested itineraries, accompanied me during drives around for photography, exploring ruins, investigating country boreens, on railway tours, in visits to pubs, and walks here and there. Some have provided lodging, others meals. There's been good conversation, considerable discussion, and the odd pint of Guinness. Thanks to everyone including: Tessa Bold, Anthony "Booster" Bools, Sean Brown of Hell's Kitchen—Castlerea, Barry & David Carse, John Cleary, the Collins family—Aobhín, Diarmaid, Gearóid, Gerry, Helen, Niamh, and Peggy—Anne Condon, Katherine Condon, Phil & Sarah Cox, Freddy the Crow, Dominick Donovan, Paul & Sarah Dowd, Liam Dunne, Noel Enright, Donal Flynn, Ken Fox, Rob Fisher, Heike Fauter, Cathy & Fiona Gunn, Mick Guilfoyle, Mark Healy, David Hegarty, Stephen Hirsch, Mark Hodge, Colin Horan, Eamon Jones, Colin Malachy, Peter Matthews, Denis McCabe, Norman McAdams, Gerry, Mooney, Dave Murphy, Colm O'Callighan, Diane O'Connell, Pius Power, Sean Ryan, Hassard Stacpoole, Kevin Walker and Ian Walsh. Thanks to the Kelly family of Tralee for hosting my first Irish visit many years ago; to Iarnród Éireann's helpful staff at many locations, including Claremorris, Enfield, Mullingar, Waterford, and Wellington Bridge. Thanks to Iarnród Éireann's Heritage Officer Gregg Ryan for a tour of the Inchicore Works. Special thanks to the Irish Railway Record Society for use of their library and answers to innumerable questions. Thanks to IRRS's members: Brian and Niall Torpey for stepping me through engineering details of Dublin Port and bridge engineering; to Tim Moriarty for details on the Irish language, Dublin history, and particulars on Irish railways; to Seamas Ratigan for detailed overviews of Irish architecture, history and politics; and to Peter Rigney for help with place names. Thanks also to everyone involved in the Railway Preservation Society for spins on their historic trains and details of Irish railway history. Contemporary culture has produced a great array of radio, film, and other types of modern media. I've been a regular listener to Today FM, finding it a great source of music, media, propaganda, news, and weather reports. The Gallery of Photography at Meeting House Square provided crucial photographic support in my early visits in Ireland. Photo Care on Abbey Street provided color film and color slide processing. And everyone at Gunn's Camera on Wexford Street took a special interest in my photography, providing me with suggestions, film, and contacts. My parents, Maureen and Richard Solomon, have visited me in Ireland, and took time to review photographs. Thanks to Simon Forty at Compendium Publishing for helping make boxes of photos and an idea into this book. I've made every effort to keep my text accurate, honest, and informative, if any errors appear they are my own.

RIGHT: Dunluce Castle's vantage point provided a stronghold from which to repel enemy attacks. The natural formation of the Giant's Causeway is a few miles to the east.

INTRODUCTION

Ireland's varied landscape ranges from the breathtaking and sublime to stark and austere. It is bucolic with rolling lush green fields, but also bleak with raised bog-land and tree-less rock-strewn mountains. Some of Ireland seems untouched by the hand of man, yet much of it displays layers of human development. From the pastoral scenes to the increasingly urban, Ireland offers much to see, enjoy and to experience. Maps make it appear deceivingly small; Ireland gets much bigger the closer you get to it. Eventually it sucks you in and before you know it you're caught in its grip.

It's been said, "Ireland makes up for its small size by the poor condition of its roads". The Irish word *bóithrín*—Anglicized as "boreen"—has become universal for a "little road". And to be sure there's no shortage of these narrow winding byways across the Irish landscape. Many are so small as to escape notice by cartographers. Yet it's the boreens that offer one the best ways to experience Ireland, if not to travel expediently across it.

The Irish coast is breathtaking. At the Cliffs of Moher, Loop Head, Slea Head, Slieve League, the Antrim Coast, and elsewhere, the land ends abruptly and endless expanse of sea extends to the horizon. Beautiful in the eyes of modern visitors, this same Irish coast was the bane of mariners over the centuries. Hidden rocks, strong currents, and fearsome cliffs were a legacy of shipwrecks and misery. Perhaps its no surprise then, that Ireland is home to some of Europe's oldest lighthouses.

Despite its difficulties, Ireland's rugged coastline provides many safe harbors, and these have attracted a legacy of interlopers and invaders. Yet one day an invader, the next a resident: Irish invaders have had an alarming propensity to settle in and become "Irish"—much to the annoyance of the Irish already living there. Exactly when the earliest human settlers arrived in Ireland has been lost to the mists of time. Evidence of intelligent civilization spans more than 7,000 years, and Ireland had some of the oldest relics of human engineering in the Western world.

RIGHT: Clare is the location of many ruined tower houses such as this one near Shannon airport. Rectangular tower houses were built in large numbers between the fourteenth and sixteenth centuries.

It is difficult to travel far in Ireland without noticing antique stone structures. It seems that virtually every town has its stone ruins—some better preserved than others, but there none-the-less. These offer a mystery, while also providing keys to the lives of the people that lived long ago. While "piles of rocks" are to hard miss, the oldest and most interesting relics must be sought out. Among the oldest and most mysterious ruins are prehistoric stone monuments called Dolmens. These are found in a variety of forms, and there are some 1,400 or more of them across the country. In many cases they are simply large standing stones, while others are more complex. Those using two enormous stones with a top cap stone are called "portal Dolmens". Most are believed to be ancient grave markers. Far more complex, but not as ancient, are the passage tombs which were built four to five thousand years ago. Most famous is Newgrange in the Boyne Valley which is hundreds of years older than the earliest Egyptian pyramids. The work of ancient engineers, this was skillfully designed to emit the first rays of the rising sun on the Winter solstice—no small feat. Another mystery are the stone circles which have been found across the British Isles. None of the extant Irish stone circles are as highly engineered or as well preserved as Stonehenge in England, many remain as evidence to a highly enlightened society, of whose thoughts and practices we no virtually nothing at all.

Although perhaps less impressive than standing stones, passage tombs, and stone rings, are large numbers of "Raths", stone or earthen ring forts—known to some as "fairy forts" that dot the countryside in the thousands. Although relatively common, these are relatively small and do not have the visual impact of Dolmens and other stone

BELOW: Uncluttered Wicklow mountain scene showing the high boggy landscape near Lough Tay.

prehistoric sites. Raths are evidence of settlements by peoples long since gone. The bit of earth and stone remaining—often under a cover of brush, moss, grass, and gorse—is all that survives of something more substantial, usually a simple dwelling.

Some antiquities are well equipped to cater for visitors. Public sites have been set up with car parks, and road signs directing the curious. At the best known and most visited sites, such as Newgrange, interpretive centers have been built, along with gift shops, tour guides, and the associated admission fees. Although this may be necessary to accommodate the flow of curiosity seekers, and helps cater to the less intrepid or less enlightened visitors, such complex accommodation has the unintentional effect of lessening the mystery and awe of the sites featured. The most intriguing antiquities are lesser known sites where ancient stones—raw

and without interpretation—can be found atop a hill in a field surrounded by sheep, or nestled in a glen with nothing more than the songs of birds to accompany them. With nothing more than chirping birds, an occasional sheep's "baah", and open sky above, the senses can lead the imagination to its own conclusions about the meaning—if not the history—of such ancient Irish relics. For those with a sense of adventure, and the willingness to seek out what few others ever see, an Ordinance Survey map can be a useful tool.

Ireland is rich with early Christian sites. By the fifth century, Christian missionaries had found their way from the continent to Ireland. The most famous is the legendary St. Patrick, Ireland's patron saint, who is believed to have traveled widely across the island and is credited with numerous feats. St. Patrick connected with the importance

of the three-leaved shamrock—with which he explained the holy-trinity—now one of the universal symbols of Ireland. In Dublin, he used a holy well to baptize converts, while at Slane he lit a fire to mark Easter, and at that high point in Co. Mayo, now known as Croagh Patrick, he famously banished snakes from Ireland. Where St. Patrick has achieved a mythic status, many extant early Christian sites across the country mark the significance of early Christian teaching in Ireland. Celtic Christianity blended pagan traditions with Christian themes producing a host of distinct symbolic and architectural evidence that remain today: the ancient Gallarous Oratory on the Dingle Peninsula dates to about the eighth century, while early Christian burial grounds and holy sites exist in many locations. Celtic High Crosses are a style closely associated with Ireland. Most were crafted during a four hundred period from the eighth century and typically installed at important holy places and monastic sites where they have weathered the ages. They are still standing at Clonmacnoise along the River Shannon in Co. Offaly, at Dysert O'Dea in Co. Clare, Glendalough in Co. Wicklow, and at Cashel, in Co. Tipperary. Some are at obscure sites, such as the Ahenny High Crosses in an old graveyard near Carrick-on-Suir in Co. Tipperary.

Monastic ruins are among the melancholy but picturesque features of the Irish countryside. Early missionaries were adept at adopting pagan sites, holidays, and symbols and integrating these things with Christian doctrines. By the sixth century, a number of important monastic sites had been founded. Growing interest in Christianity became intrinsic to Irish life for centuries and resulted in construction of numerous extensive monastic sites across the island. At one time these were important fixtures of political and spiritual power as

well as repositories of considerable knowledge and wealth. The roll of Irish monks in copying, and thus preserving, classical literature has been well documented. Among Ireland's greatest treasures are the surviving books from the dark ages, such as the famous *Book of Kells* at Trinity College. Many of the monastic sites have not fared as well. Since the ninth century they were favored targets of Viking raiders, who recognized the value of monastic wealth, if not the knowledge and spirituality of the Christian faith. As protection from such raids, tall, narrow, round towers were

RIGHT: One of the Ahenny high crosses, County Tipperary. Ahenny boasts two crosses, among the earliest in Ireland, each filled with geometrical motifs so similar to the Book of Kells that they are attributed to the same period—the 8th century. *David Lyons*

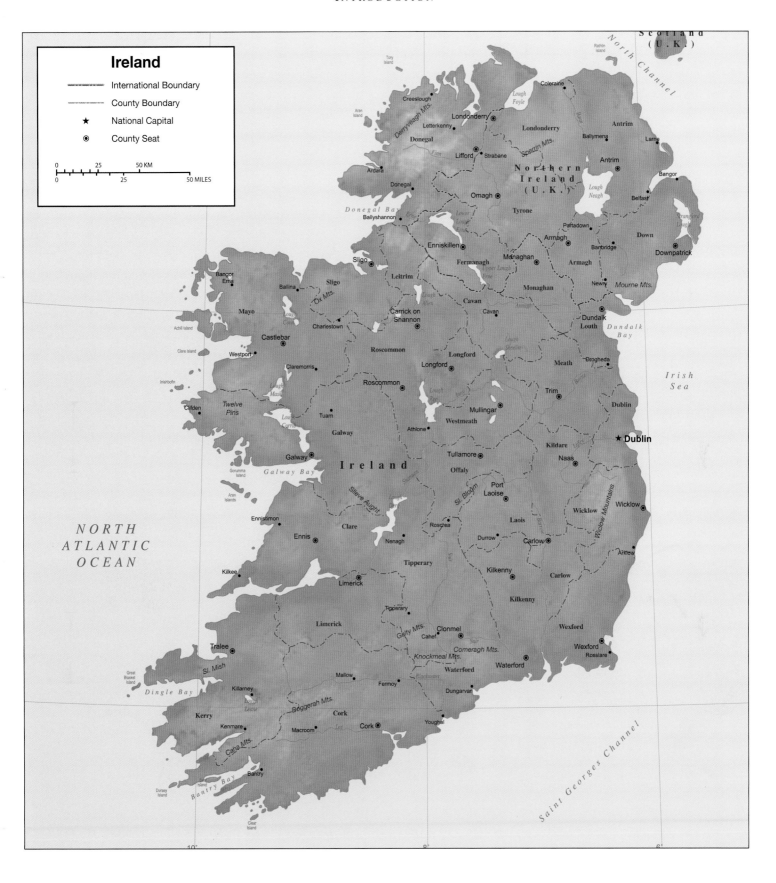

Ireland

- ——— International Boundary
- —·—·— County Boundary
- ★ National Capital
- ◉ County Seat

constructed. Often at least ninety feet tall, these towers served to protect precious manuscripts, as well as providing human refuge during Norse rampages and other times of strife. With the doors well above ground level, and a smooth tapered exterior, round towers seemed to provide a safe haven for those people and treasures sequestered inside. Yet, they were conceived before the invention of the canon and many didn't last as a result of later wars. However a great many round towers still survive. Round towers were only

one element of Irish monasteries but are one of their most distinctive features. Catholic monastic sites were suppressed in the fifteenth century under King Henry VIII. Yet some continued to thrive until the Cromwellian wars of the mid-seventeenth century when many were destroyed. Surviving ruins are the legacy of these campaigns.

Ireland's violent medieval history is recalled by the large number of stone fortifications that dot the countryside. Popular visions of lords and ladies conjured up by nineteenth century romantics rarely convey any truth about Irish castles. They were built in difficult times by men with means, and too often were the scene of wanton bloodshed during political struggles. Some castles are substantial affairs dating from the Anglo-Norman invasion. Of these, Trim Castle along the River Boyne in Co. Meath is the largest and most imposing. Others are awe-inspiring because of their location; Dunluce Castle, Co. Antrim straddles a narrow promontory on a high cliff directly above the crashing waves of the Atlantic. However, most common are the tall, narrow, rectangular tower houses built in large numbers between the fourteenth and sixteenth centuries. The more strategic of these were fortifications built in anticipation of invasion, but most were residences for land-controlling families. Tower houses are found across Ireland, but are most common in the south Midlands, and across Wexford, Waterford, Clare, and Cork. The size and orientation of tower house varies, but the essential pattern remains fairly consistent. Most were three or four stories tall. At the bottom, windows are little more than narrow slits. Typically a dining area was located on the ground floor, with sleeping quarters and storage areas higher up. As with many stone structures, extant tower houses and other castles are often just surviving remnants of something greater. The stones are like bleached bones of a long dead beast. Looking at them

we can get a sense for what they were about, but are afforded little detail to what they were like when occupied. Frequently, tower houses were attached to other structures and served only as a refuge during times of danger. Also, while we see them as dull gray stone structures, most appeared quite differently several hundred years ago. Outer surfaces were protected and appeared white rather than gray. The interiors were finished with wood and made livable. Restored structures such as the fifteenth century O'Donnell Castle in Donegal town provide a better sense for what the tower houses may have been like inside. Yet, while a handful of castles are restored, and some open to the public, many more are little more than forlorn ruins standing in a field where they may shelter livestock or provide a home to crows, and little else. Some appear nearly intact, others clearly reveal the signs of siege. The poet W.B. Yeats, bought an old tower house in 1916, in rural Galway and made it his home. Today this tower, known as Thoor Ballylee, is a museum that is open seasonally to the public for an admission fee.

Prior to the arrival of the Vikings in the eighth century, there were no large towns in Ireland. People tended to live in small settlements and wee villages scattered across the countryside. As a result, few towns in Ireland can trace their lineage back more than about 1,200 years and the oldest are

LEFT: An old Guinness advertisement at Anascaul, Co. Kerry promotes virtues of this popular stout.

ABOVE: Wind off the Atlantic whistles as sheep gnaw the windswept grass of the Dingle Peninsula on Slea Head.

known Viking settlements such as Dublin, Drogheda, Wexford, and Waterford. Most towns developed after the Anglo-Norman invasions. Some, such as Cahir, Co. Tipperary, formed around castles. Cahir is the anglicized version of the Irish word *Cathair* that means a stone enclosure. Other towns formed around natural features, such as river fords and these may predate both Viking and Norman invasions, but when they were settled is conjectural. Irish town names often reveal a bit of history—although names have typically been anglicized (and in some cases changed altogether). Athy, Co. Kildare along the River Barrow, takes its name from the Irish *Átha* for "ford". This root word is common to many Irish town names. Athenry (Co. Galway) is derived from *Átha an Rí*, "the ford of the kings"; Athlone comes from *Átha Luain*, "Luan's ford"; Ballina come from *Béal an Átha*, the 'mouth of the ford'. (However some translators indicate that in the case of Ballina, Co. Mayo, the name infers "ford of the mouth of the wood".) The village of Ballinamuck, translates to "ford of the pigs".

There are many other common threads in Irish town names. *Baile* is an Irish word for a settlement, be it a dwelling, village, or other type of inhabited place. This has been anglicized as Bally, and often applied to place names as "town" or "ton" would be in English. Sometimes this done in a literal and descriptive fashion such as Ballysallagh, which means "dirtytown". In other situations "bally" is combined with an historic figure or the name of someone who lived there, such as Ballyferriter, Co. Kerry, which takes its name from the ruins of the historical figure Pairas Ferriter who had a castle here, and is legendary for his stand against Cromwell's armies. Common Irish words frequently incorporated into names and anglicized include: *carraig*, "carrick"—translates as "rock or a large noteworthy stone"; *cluain*, anglicized as "clon" or "cloon"—means "meadow"; *dún*, becomes "dun"—means "fort"; *muileann* becomes "mullin"—meaning "mill", as in *Mulleann Cearr*—Mullingar (Co. West Meath); *ráth* becomes "rath"—as described earlier this an "earthen foundation or fort", a structure sometimes known as "fairy fort". Translations and Anglicizations have lead to confusion. For example the Irish adapted the Latin *cella* into *cill*, which can be taken as a church or simply as a monastic location. This word has often been anglicized as "kill" or "kil", as in Kildare for *Cildara*—which means "Church of the Oak Tree". However, confusion may arise from translation of the Irish word *coill* which means a "wood" (as in a forest), yet has also be anglicized as "kil".

Maps tend to only show the larger places. Yet, virtually every place in Ireland has been given a name. Every crossroads, copse of trees, escarpment or rise in the land, every inlet, every stream, and just about any place man has settled has its name. These names are not necessarily unique to the place, and in fact are often duplicated. How many places are called "Gort"—which means "field"? Back when few people strayed too far from where they were born, it made little difference if some other county had a place with the same name. Even some fairly large towns sometimes used the same name; there's a town called Dungarvin in both Co. Kilkenny, and in Co. Waterford. Yet for all these names there are remarkably few signs in Ireland. Some wee place along the side of a road may have carried a name for centuries, and yet there will be nothing proclaiming it. However, all the locals will know the name, and you might be expected to know it as well!

RIGHT: A storm brews, and waves batter Portally Cove along the Waterford Coast near Dunmore East.

DUBLIN

BELOW: Looking east down toward the "James Joyce" bridge on Christmas Morning 2005. Designed by architects Santiago Calatravells with input from Dublin's Roughan & O'Donovan, this is one of the newest Liffey bridges.

DUBLIN

These days, Ireland's largest city and capital of the Republic seems to have taken a cosmopolitan streak, and has more in common with Europe than the rest of Ireland. But this really isn't a new trend and in fact it is intrinsic to Dublin's history. The city's foreign connections are key to its legacy.

When it was that the first people settled in Dublin predates all written records, but it is known that a Gaelic Irish community existed here centuries ago. A ford across the River Liffey, known as the Átha Cliath, lent Dublin its first Irish name, *Baile Átha Cliath*—"the town of the ford of hurdles"—by which it is still known in Irish. Dublin began attracting Europeans a long time ago. The Vikings found it by the year 840, settled in and made use of its harbor as a raiding base. They found that a short distance east of *Átha Cliath*, near the confluence of the Liffey and a winding stream called the Poddle, was an inky pond suitable to moor their longships. Here they set up camp, and stayed for centuries. The locals called this pond *Dubh Linn,* which translates to "Black Pool". The Vikings called this Dyflin. Over the years the settlement that developed here came to be known in English as "Dublin".

As Dublin grew and expanded, the port that began at the very center of the community was gradually pushed further and further down river, and ultimately out into Dublin Bay. Long before this happened, the Vikings had intermarried with the Irish and formed a Hiberno-Norse culture that was more Irish than Norse. Despite their reputation as fearsome

BELOW: Trinity College's *Campanile* seen after heavy rain. Built between 1852 and 1853, this distinctive structure is located at the center of Trinity's Parliament Square and credited to Sir Charles Lanyon.

RIGHT: Among Dublin's landmarks is the Trinity College gate facing College Green. The gate dates to between 1755 and 1759 and features classical Corinthian style.

warriors, power struggles within Ireland saw an end to Viking domination in the eleventh century. Irish armies, led by the ambitious Brian Boru, fought the Vikings in a conclusive battle at Clontarf in 1014. Boru perished in this battle, but the Vikings' power had been checked. Although the Hiberno-Irish largely stayed, control of the land shifted back to Irish chieftains. This changed in 1170, when a local dispute led a disenfranchized Irish chieftain to hire Anglo-Norman mercenaries to aid his cause. Knights arrived en masse from England, under the leadership of Strongbow. They quickly established a presence in Ireland and were largely based at Dublin and Trim. To ensure they remained loyal, King Henry II of England took measures that forged a bond between Ireland and England which lasted centuries.

Because of its strategic location, Dublin emerged as the foremost Anglo-Norman settlement in Ireland. A substantial moated castle was built near the site of the old Black Pool, and a walled medieval city was constructed to the west of the castle. The struggles between the established Hiberno-Irish, Gaelic Irish, and Anglo-Norman conquerors have filled many books. Over time, the Anglo-Normans, like the Vikings before them, began to adopt Irish manners, speech, and habits. After a few centuries, they were nearly as Irish as everyone else on the island.

Plagues struck from time to time, decimating the city's population, as elsewhere in Europe. Yet the city of Dublin kept growing. At first, primary settlement had been on the south bank of the Liffey, as the north bank was less desirable because of marshy land. When the Anglo-Norman's established their presence and built their castle on the south bank, the Hiberno-Norse and others resettled across the river to a place that became known as Oxmantown.

For centuries greater Dublin and its environs were known to the ruling class as "The Pale", which they viewed as a bastion of civilization, beyond which was an unruly, uncivilized, and dangerous country. Reaffirming this belief were periodic raids on Norman forts and walls by "wild" Gaelic Irish. Today these raids are still symbolized by the age old Dublin coat of arms featuring three burning castles. Close ties between England and Ireland resulted in England's feuds spilling over to Ireland from time to time. Gradually England's grip on Ireland tightened. England's wars in the mid-seventeenth century became Ireland's problems. Following the destructive Cromwellian period, Dublin, entered a golden period of development. In the later half of the seventeenth century, The Duke of Ormonde, Lord Lieutenant of Dublin began the process altering the shape of the city according to an enlightened vision. Where the medieval city had grown in a haphazard manner gradually spilling over its walls, creating neighborhoods beyond the old city, from the late seventeenth century onward, Dublin's growth was directed

BELOW: Ducks enjoy a fountain at St. Stephen's Green. The Green was enclosed in the seventeenth century, made into a public park by Arthur Guinness, great grandson of the Guinness brewery founder of the same name.

and planned. Ormonde desired that Dublin follow a Parisian model, and land along the Liffey was reclaimed, and new quays built to channel the river. These were kept open and made into broad new streets rather than allowing buildings to be built right along the water front. Four new Liffey bridges were built in the course of fourteen years beginning in 1670. This enabled intensive residential development on the north side of the river. The castle was remodeled, with new structures that absorbed the old Anglo-Norman walls into a much changed building that better suited contemporary administration of the city.

The eighteenth century saw Dublin attain a basic street plan, largely still in place today in the city center. Wealthy, influential families bought and developed lands around the old city. By mid-century, rapid development and growth resulted in the old city becoming clogged with unmanageable traffic as horses, carriages, people on foot, and street traders all vied for space within the narrow confines of medieval alleys and winding streets. The chaotic arrangement of buildings didn't help matters at all. In 1757, the Wide Streets Commission was established to solve Dublin's planning inadequacies, and established building standards and put into place new thoroughfares which provide Dublin with a world class urban environment. Over the next century, Dublin installed new broad streets, set practical and aesthetical standards for new construction, and rearranged areas of the old city previously plagued by poor planning. Among the noteworthy developments of this period were the four classical Georgian Squares, partly modeled on the development around the St. Stephen's Green southeast of the old city. This one-time public common had been transformed into an exclusive new neighborhood in the last half of the seventeenth century. Although smaller, the Georgian squares emulated this plan, with an open green space and standardized terraced houses built all around. Still admired today, Mountjoy, Parnell (formerly Rutland), Merrion, and Fitzwilliam Squares were the epitome of affluent Georgian Dublin.

The plan for new dwellings, now described as the Georgian terrace house, required that buildings share common external characteristics and used a common line of frontage. Yet subtle variation was encouraged, that insured within the uniform plan each house exhibited individual character.

Dublin's political roll was drastically changed as the city was being remodeled in the Georgian style. Events relating to both the American and French Revolutions, produced an Irish uprising in 1798, the consequence of which saw the end

LEFT: Designed by Sir Edward Lovett Pearce, this classic structure at College Green was for the Irish Parliament, but has served the Bank of Ireland since the early nineteenth century.

of Dublin's role as Ireland's capital when government functions were relocated to London. Implications for Dublin were complex: the trail of power and money abandoned the city, which entered a period of financial decline. The advent of the Great Famine in the 1840s saw Dublin's population swell with impoverished people from the countryside seeking relief, work, or transport overseas. With the influx of the rural poor, Dublin's urban environs became increasingly unappealing to affluent middle and upper classes. They gradually moved away from the city center to new townships at the edge of the city. Dublin's city center became a commercial area ringed by seething slums. While long known for its poorer quarters, such as the old Liberties west of St. Patrick's cathedral, in the later half of the nineteenth century many once posh Georgian Terrace houses were subdivided as tenements. Whole areas of the city once known as the homes to the Ascendency became impoverished slums where large numbers of people were squashed together in filthy conditions.

The combined effects from Dublin's worsening slums, growing political unrest and a political desire for the return to "home rule", along with interest in the Gaelic cultural revival came to a head during the first decades of the twentieth century. The famous Easter Rising of 1916 set the wheels in motion for an Independent Ireland. Following two years of war, in 1921, the six northern counties were separated by partition to form Northern Ireland which remained part of the United Kingdom. Unhappy with this arrangement Civil War ensued, following a truce in 1923, and the twenty-six southern counties became the Irish Free State, governed from Dublin. For the first time in more than a century, Dublin was again a capital city but the transition had not been easy. The question of the Partition remained controversial, and only in the last ten years have these issues attained a level of political calm.

Dublin entered a new phase. Ireland, although politically independent, remained economically tied to Great Britain. Economic problems plagued independent Ireland in its early years. The country was neutral during the Second World War, and after the war the Irish Free State became the Republic of Ireland, yet for years investment remained at starvation levels. Inner city Dublin was still saddled with poverty and urban decay. Some new construction during the 1950s and 1960s resulted in new buildings in the city center, while suburban development outside the center produced many new homes, however the old Georgian city was largely stagnant. It seemed a ghost of another era.

Change came as the result of several fundamental efforts. Ireland joined the European Economic Community in the 1970s, now the European Union, and coalescing postwar Europe provided a high level of investment previously unattainable in Ireland. This, combined with growing globalization and the propensity of American companies to locate offices and facilities outside the United States, favored Ireland and greatly benefited Dublin. Ireland's advantageous tax laws, comparatively streamlined bureaucracy and its highly educated, English-speaking population have made Ireland—especially Dublin—an ideal location for many American businesses. Irish tourism, vigorously promoted in the lean years, also had an important role.

Ireland's economy picked up quickly in the 1990s, producing a dynamic transformation known as the Celtic Tiger. Since then Dublin has seemed to be one huge building site with substantial construction and development across the city center as well as in the ever growing suburbs. In a short time, Dublin has become one of the most vibrant cities in Europe. Low unemployment has contributed to producing a thriving multi-cultural environment as people of all races from around the world have made Dublin their home. Today's Dublin retains a background defined by its Georgian glory years, while thriving as an ever changing modern cosmopolitan hotspot.

RIGHT: Statue of James Joyce on Talbot Street looking toward O'Connell Street. Joyce's literature preserved the character of the city and considered by many to be part of Dublin.

PAGES 28–29: The choir of St. Patrick's Cathedral, Dublin. The cathedral is the largest church in Ireland and has its origins in 450 when it is said that the saint baptized converts around here. Today, it is the national cathedral of the Protestant Church of Ireland. The banners, symbolic swords, and helmets are those of the Order of St.Patrick. This was founded in 1783 to reward Irish peers and those in high office in Ireland—as the Garter did in England and the Thistle in Scotland. The order effectively went into abeyance with the establishment of the Irish Free State in 1922 and lapsed completely in 1974 with the death of the last surviving recipient, Prince Henry, Duke of Gloucester. *David Lyons*

LEFT: Statues in the North Aisle of St. Patrick's Cathedral, Dublin. From left to right: Archbishop Jones, Dean Dawson, Buckingham, Whiteside. St. Patrick's was started in the late 12th and early 13th centuries and most of it was built between 1254 and 1270. The spire was added in the 18th century. Jonathan Swift, author of Gulliver's Travels, was dean here from 1713 to 1745. *David Lyons*

PAGES 32–33: St. Patrick's Day is a national holiday and Dublin sponsors fireworks; viewed here from the River Liffey looking east toward the Ha' Penny (Liffey) and O'Connell Bridges.

ABOVE: Rowan Gillespie's *Famine Monument* was installed on Custom House Quay in 1997. The haunted figures convey the destitution, hopelessness and pain of famine sufferers.

RIGHT ABOVE: A grave contrast of prosperity and famine: Gillespie's *Famine Monument* and Custom House Quay are seen against a backdrop of container lorries and the modern Irish Financial Services Centre.

RIGHT BELOW: Symbols of Ireland: The Irish tricolor snaps in the wind over the General Post Office on a sunny clear Christmas morning. James Connolly what would you think?

BELOW: Lighthouse at Howth and rocky barren
Eye of Ireland island beyond.

LEFT: Martello Tower on Ireland's Eye, a small islet just out of Howth, today a bird sanctuary. The Martello towers were defensive measures against a possible French invasion set up in the late 18th and early 19th centuries. The name comes from a tower on Mortella Point, Corsica, that put up a good fight when British sea and land forces were sent to take it in 1794. *David Lyons*

BELOW: Europe's largest obelisk, known officially as the Wellington Testimonial, is in the distance on the left within Dublin's Phoenix Park—the largest enclosed city park in Europe.

LEFT: Constructed to honor the Duke of Wellington born in Dublin; this monumental obelisk was begun in 1819 but not completed until 1864. It is seen after a heavy rain with a bright rainbow.

RIGHT: The artistic vision of London's Ian Ritchie, The Spire on O'Connell Street was completed in January 2003. Measuring 120 meters, it is by far Dublin's tallest public monument.

BELOW: Reflection of buildings along the North Quays west of St. Pauls at Smithfield. Arch bridge. Four Courts in the distance (right).

PAGES 60–61: Sun glints off the cobbles along Temple Bar. Named for Sir William Temple, when the "Bar" was the riverfront in the seventeenth century. Today the Liffey is a block to the north.

ABOVE: On the Liffey's North Quays, the Four
Courts basks in the summer sun. Completed in
1802, Ireland's High Court was among the many
Dublin accomplishments of English-born architect
James Gandon.

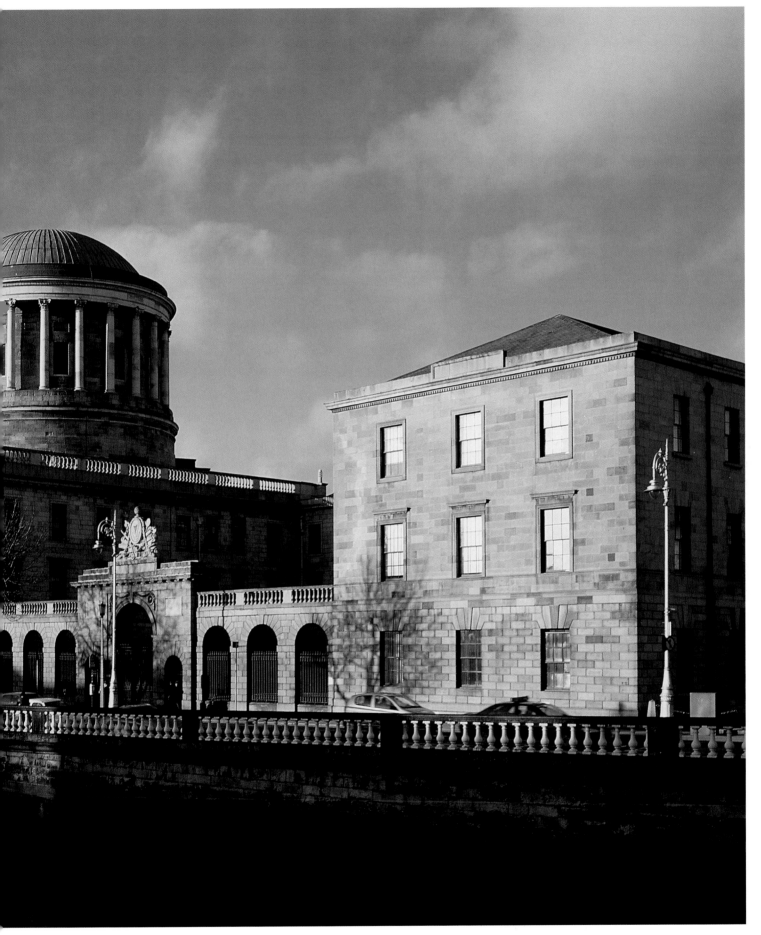

PAGES 64–65: Synod Hall footbridge connects its namesake with Christ Church by spanning Dublin's Winetavern Street. Although portions of Christ Church date to medieval times, this gothic-style bridge and much of the extant church are nineteenth century improvements.

LEFT: Sunset on the South Circular Road looking toward Leonard's Corner.

ABOVE: A translation of Irish word *Luas* is "speed", an apt name for the new tram system that opened in 2004. LUAS crosses the specifically built asymmetrical cable-stayed Taney Bridge at Dundrum.

RIGHT: Located in Dublin's trendy Temple Bar area, Irish musicians play at the *Auld Dub*. Outside a chalk sign beckons custom with the words "Irish music every afternoon and evening".

BELOW: The mouth of the Liffey at Dublin Port. Stacks from the Poolbeg Generating Station loom above pleasure boats and container ships.

PREVIOUS PAGE: Under and over at Abbey Street: on a bright April afternoon, Irish Rail's "DART" glides between Connolly and Tara Street as a "LUAS" tram hums down Abbey Street.

RIGHT: The Grand Canal looking from Leeson Street Bridge to Macartney Bridge and Baggot Street, Dublin. *David Lyons*

SUNNY SOUTHEAST
WICKLOW, WATERFORD AND WEXFORD

of the combined Rivers Suir and Barrow. The tip of this long peninsula extends into the Celtic Sea, is home to an twelfth century Anglo-Norman lighthouse—believed to be one the oldest operating lighthouses in Europe. It can be seen flashing its warning for many miles.

County Waterford, takes its name from the city of the same name which, like Wexford, was a significant Viking port from the ninth century. Waterford city, is located on the shores of the River Suir a considerable distance upriver from the Celtic Sea, yet because of the great depth of the

BELOW: Streets of Waterford at night. A hint of blue in the sky.

estuary, has remained an important Irish port. Traditionally Waterford was used to import timber, grain, cement and coal, while exporting largely agricultural produce and livestock. Waterford's large quayside has been adapted for modern shipping. The container port located at Belview on the Kilkenny side of the Suir a few miles east of Waterford is the most important port facility.

Waterford city still retains a number of stone towers from its old Viking and medieval city wall. Prominent on the waterfront is Reginald's Tower on the east side of the city centre. Named for Reginald the Dane, this impressive circular stone edifice, dates to the early Anglo-Norman conquest of the city. Many Waterford streets follow a medieval layout, making wandering through town an exercise in ending up some place other than where intended. The town retains a certain edge as a result of its eighteenth and nineteenth century industrial character. It is well known as the home of Waterford Crystal which is manufactured south of the city. Established in 1783 by the Penrose family, the present Waterford Crystal is a modern organization resulting from a mid-twentieth century revival. West of the city centre on the south bank of the Suir is a modern Guinness Brewery that augments the brewery's primary facility at St. James's Gate in Dublin, and primarily brews for export. On the north side of the Suir are Iarnród Éireann's (Irish Rail) yards and station in an area artificially grafted to Co. Waterford that would naturally be part of Co. Kilkenny. The aesthetically challenged Lego-block style passenger station and office dates to the 1960s, and is one of the few instances of a modern building replacing a

traditional structure. In 2008, the railway had plans to replace the building again, hopefully this time with something more pleasing to look at. As the junction of several lines, Waterford is one of the more important Irish railway terminals.

On the south Waterford coast are two greatly contrasting seaside towns. Dunmore East on the shore of Waterford Harbor was a small port and fishing village. This tidy town, nestled along red cliffs over looking the water, features a small sandy beach, separated from its own sheltered harbor. A number of nicely preserved traditional thatched cottages, an unusual thatched roof pub, along with a handful of restaurants and shops has made this quiet town a desirable rural retreat. Tramore, located just a few miles west along the coast on the west side of a broad bay, is significantly larger and features a long broad sandy beach from which the town gets its name. This has developed as a popular summer seaside destination for working-class Dubliners and other urban Irish seeking sun, sand and entertainment. In the high season, its pubs and gaming arcades are thronged with enthusiastic holidaymakers; in winter the atmosphere is more subdued. At one time, Tramore was served by its own railway line, unusual because it was completely isolated from the rest of Ireland's railway network. This was lifted decades ago and all visitors must now crowd the two-lane roads from Waterford to reach the town.

BELOW: Ragwort and purple loosestrife, Saltee Islands, County Wexford. *Davis Lyons*

BELOW: The sometimes quiet back streets of
Waterford town looking toward *The Munster* pub.

BELOW: Ruined church and churchyard opposite
the river from Dungarvin, Co. Waterford.

BELOW: The Causeway Bridge at Dungarvin, Co. Waterford consists of a seventy-seven foot six inch span over the River Colligan. It is unusual among Irish bridges because it was built with Cheshire sandstone.

BELOW: The view north of New Ross, County Wexford, and the valley of the River Barrow from the summit of Slieve Coilte where the 1798 rebels camped, June 7–10. *David Lyons*

ABOVE: Looking out over the Atlantic from a rocky head Portally Cove near Dunmore East, Co. Waterford.

RIGHT: November sunrise near Dunmore East. The lighthouse at Hook Head, Co. Wexford warns ships off the rocks. Hook Head is famous for the saying "by hook and by crook".

BELOW: Old fishermen's cottages near Dunmore East make for pleasant summer homes. Thatched roofs are an added attraction and make for nice photos but can bring creepy surprises for unaware sleepers when bugs fall unannounced from the thatch.

BELOW: Colorful fishing boats rest in the harbor at Dunmore East, Co. Waterford.

BELOW: Fishing boats at Cheekpoint with the famous Barrow Bridge beyond. Built in 1906, this 14 span Pratt truss is the largest railway bridge in Ireland.

PAGES 96–97: Established by the Vikings in the ninth century, Waterford remains an important Irish port today, and is the only active port on the island where international containers are transloaded from ship to rail.

ABOVE: Beautifully maintained thatched roof cottages near the beach at Dunmore East, Co. Waterford.

RIGHT: A statuette of an angel catches the light in the graveyard for the Church of Ireland St. Andrews Church at Dunmore East, Co. Waterford.

ABOVE: The pristine Upper Lake at Glendalough contributes to the site being a popular place for visitors. St. Kevin who founded the church here is supposed to have lived an ascetic existence for more than a century.

RIGHT: Trees in silhouette at Sally Gap, Wicklow Mountains at the boggy headwaters of the River Liffey.

ABOVE: The River Dargle cascades down a 425 foot cliff to form the Powerscourt Waterfall. This is among several popular scenic attractions in Co. Wicklow, less than an hour's drive from Dublin.

BELOW: Mountain goats in the Wicklow mountains at a barren and windswept rise near Lough Tay.

RIGHT: Uncluttered Wicklow mountain scene showing the high boggy landscape near Lough Tay.

ABOVE: The old Dublin & South Eastern railway station catches the sun at Newcastle, Co. Wicklow. The Dirty Slow & Easy is long just a memory. And while Irish Rail trains pass now and again, they no longer stop for passengers.

BELOW AND ABOVE RIGHT: Running toward Dublin Railway Preservation Society of Ireland excursion train led by Dublin & South Eastern locomotive 461 runs along the beach along the Irish Sea at Newcastle, Co. Wicklow.

BELOW RIGHT: Winter view of tree trunks near the Powerscourt Waterfall.

PAGES 110–111: Along the Barrow/Suir estuary at the village of Arthurstown, Co. Wexford a stone castle dating from about the fifteenth century catches the afternoon sun. Many towns were built around protective fortification.

RIGHT: Fishing trawler *Harvest Seeker* is at the Quays in Arthurstown, Co. Wexford along the Barrow/Suir estuary.

LEFT: "United Irishmen" by Eamonn O'Doherty on the New Ross–Wexford road. There was an action here against Wexford garrison forces on May 30, 1798, during Wolfe Tone's rising. O'Doherty is one of Ireland's most famous public artists whose work may be seen in many of its major cities—Dublin has his sculpture depicting Anna Livia Plurabelle (the "Floozie in the Jacuzzi"). Other pieces of large-scale public sculpture are to be found in Galway, Antrim, Dun Laoghaire, Enniskillen, Cobh, and Navan. Other commissions include the Great Hunger Memorial in Westchester, New York. *David Lyons*

RIGHT: The Norman Black Castle guards the harbor entrance to Wicklow. The castle was begun by Maurice Fitzgerald when he was granted the district in 1176, but his death a year later delayed its completion. The castle was frequently attacked by the Irish and sometimes occupied by them. Early in the 16th century it was held by the O'Brynes, but they had to surrender to the Crown in 1543. Luke O'Toole invested the fortress in 1641, but was forced to raise the siege when the British Army arrived. *David Lyons*

BELOW: A Railway Preservation Society of Ireland excursion train whistles to warn pedestrians as it works down Wexford Quay in thick coastal fog. Wexford is among historic towns established by the Vikings more than a thousand years ago.

BELOW: In May 2004, Iarnród Éireann's afternoon Waterford to Rosslare passenger train can be seen to the left of Dunbrody Abbey near Campile, Co. Wexford.

LEFT: Gothic arched doorways and stone walls speak of an earlier era at Dunbrody Abbey, Co. Wexford. Established by Hervé de Montmorency in the twelfth century, it was largely constructed between the thirteenth and fifteenth centuries.

ABOVE: Afternoon sun illuminates the stone ruins of the old Cistercian Dunbrody Abbey near Campile, Co. Wexford.

PAGES 120–121: Vestiges of glory: a ruined wall reaches skyward as the sun peaks below the fast moving clouds of a brisk winter sky at Dunbrody Abbey, Co. Wexford.

PAGES 124–125: View east over the River Barrow to the town center, New Ross, County Wexford. *David Lyons*

CORK & KERRY

BELOW: A rooftop view of Cobh and surrounding harbor, with distant hills on the far bank of the Lee estuary. Cobh is situated on Great Island, the largest island in the Lee, and location of the largest port and harbor facilities in south west Ireland.

CORK & KERRY

erry's wild and lush landscape has a greater resonance than its towns. Its rugged rocky sea coast is characterized by large peninsulas jutting into the North Atlantic and home to fishermen, farmers, and some of Ireland's largest-surviving Irish speaking communities. Language in Kerry is enigmatic; to outsiders even the soft spoken English can be difficult to understand. More challenging is the native tongue that has survived in pockets in Kerry for centuries. In places, road signs are strictly in Irish, lending a charm to the place, but making navigation challenging. "*Go Mall*" on road signs or painted on the pavement is a warning and *not* a commercial shopping promotion. Tralee is Kerry's largest town, its center comprised of a maze of streets lined with shops, pubs, restaurants and hotels. A thriving place, its environs tell little of the scenic splendor that lie beyond it to the southwest. Years ago, Tralee was the terminal of Ireland's most remarkable rural railway, the narrow gauge Tralee & Dingle, that connected its namesake towns via a steep and perilous route over the Dingle Peninsula. Largely a cattle hauler in its last years, the much loved little railway was abandoned in the early 1950s following years of infrequent, intermittent operation, and long before the Dingle Peninsula developed any significant tourist interest. If the line still operated today it would be among Ireland's leading attractions. In recent years, a very short segment of the old T&D was rebuilt between Tralee and nearby Blennerville, but this is a seasonal attraction designed to entertain visitors

rather than provide transport. However, travelers of the main road to Dingle town will spot vestiges of the old T&D line and viaducts.

Kerry's isolated Dingle Peninsula is among Ireland's great treasures. Narrow cliff side roads offer stunning vistas of the Blasket Islands from steep tree-less slopes on Slea Head. The remote windswept Blaskets are now uninhabited, but until 1953 were occupied by a small but hardy population. In those times, Tralee was a far and distant town, and Dublin seemed like the other side of the world. Significant pre-historic architecture are among the attractions of the Dingle Peninsula. Fahan Beehive huts, perhaps built as solitary quarters for meditating monks or visiting pilgrims, dot the slopes near Slea Head. Now shelter for the occasion sheep, it is difficult to comprehend the sparse, ascetic, and difficult lives of the human occupants of these modest structures. The Gallarus Oratory, near the village of Ballyferriter— *Baile an Fheirtéaraigh,* is considered Ireland's oldest, and best kept early Christian place of worship. Few if any records exist to establish its date of construction, but it may

be have been built as early as the sixth century. With just two openings—the door and a small window at the back— the interior is dark and unadorned.

Another regional contrast with the villages and rugged seaside scenery of Dingle is Killarney town which was developed from the eighteenth century to cater to visitors to the bucolic lakes and mountains nearby—now the Killarney National Park. To the southwest are the famed MacGillycuddy's Reeks—the tallest mountains in Ireland, due south is Mangerton Mountain, and to the southeast is Crohane Mountain and beyond are the Derrynasaggart Mountains. A significant rocky cleft in the MacGillycuddy's called the Gap of Dunloe is popular with hill walkers and visitors, but not with local motorists who must exercise exceptional care negotiating the sinuous boreen that passes as a road. The narrow confines of the pass combined with

BELOW: Cork's Cape Clear Island; remote and desolate beauty, sinuous single lane road leads toward the North Atlantic coast, a ruined castle in the distance.

the unusual hues of the surrounding mountainsides and the propensity of the mountains to provide their own dynamic micro-climate makes for a natural light show and continuously changing landscape vista. Sun and low cloud sculpt ever new shapes and present arrays of colors on the rocky peaks. Lough Leane is key to the network of fresh water southwest of Killarney town. Its shores are dotted with vestiges of past human inhabitation. Among these are ancient copper mines, the ruins of Ross Castle, and the remnants of Muckross Friary—built in the fifteenth century and destroyed in the seventeenth.

Beyond Killarney lies another of Kerry's most famous places, the Iveragh Peninsula, better known by the colloquial name for the road that that wraps around its shores, the "Ring of Kerry". This may be accessed by way of Killorglin to the west, or to the south over the spectacular Moll's Gap—reached on a tortuous two-lane road that passes through one of Ireland's few old road tunnels. Views of the Skellig Islands off the southern coast of the Iveragh Peninsula give a hint of what these rocky refuges are like. Skellig Michael, once home to pious monks living at a seventh century monastic settlement which includes clusters of rocky Beehive Huts, now has no human habitation, although may be visited in the summer months by intrepid tourists. These islands are known for their thriving populations of Gannets and Puffins who live among the rocky crags. Caherciveen on the north shore of the peninsula facing Dingle Bay is known as the birth place of Daniel O'Connell, the skilled Irish politician who brought about Catholic emancipation in the nineteenth century, and one-time Lord Mayor of Dublin, for whom O'Connell Street and O'Connell Bridge were named. Most of the village is laid out along the main road. It's a haven for traditional musicians, and was once reached by another of Kerry's spectacular railway lines, now long abandoned. At the bottom of the peninsula is Kenmare, lovely Irish town along the estuary of the same name.

Cork city is by far the most populated place in the county of the same name. Cork city is to the county, like Dublin is to the rest of Ireland; it is the biggest urban conurbation but bears little resemblance to the greater countryside. The city is visually impressive with its center set on a sizable island in the River Lee, with residential neighborhoods clinging to steeply rising hills north and south of the river. A long-time industrial haven, Cork city makes for a blend of gritty twentieth century factories and waterfront businesses with splendid pubs, hotels, restaurants and neat city parks. Where Dublin has long been home to Guinness stout, Cork has two well known breweries, Beamish and Murphy's, whose local stouts are preferred by locals. A suburban railway connects Cork with nearby Cobh (pronounced "Cove") by way of Fota Island—home to a splendid zoo. Cobh was formerly known as Queenstown,

and the location of a significant deepwater harbor, best remembered as the final port of call for the *Titanic* before its untimely meeting with an iceberg. Cobh village features a large cathedral and colorfully painted buildings. The old railway terminal was once one of the most important in Ireland. From here the mail was dispatched to and received from America and Canada. Many of the Irish, dispossessed as result of the Great Famine, left Ireland through Cobh, taking final one-way railway journeys from their rural towns to ships waiting for them here. Very few ever returned. The railway station is now a popular museum.

West Cork comprises the bulk of County Cork, Ireland's largest. There are a number of quaint villages and towns, among them Kinsale, Skibbereen, Skull, Baltimore and Bantry. Off the coast are a few populated islands reached by

regularly scheduled ferries. One of the largest is Clear Island, notable for its Gaeltacht—Irish speaking community. This stark largely tree-less island is a raw, yet fascinating environment. Mizen Head, Ireland's southwesterly most point, is reachable by a narrow bridge. This rocky isolated point is battered by storms that blow in along the Jet Stream and as a result Mizen Head is regularly featured in Irish weather reports.

Undoubtedly Cork's most famous attraction, if not its most interesting, is Blarney Castle, where unwary tourists have long been coaxed into kissing the Blarney Stone. The ruins of the thirteenth century Timoleague Abbey near Clonkilty have a charming but melancholy air about them. Like so many Christian ruins in Ireland, these suffered as result of wars in the mid-seventeenth century.

BELOW: Fishing trawler in the harbor at Cape Clear Island.

BELOW: The ruined fourteenth century friary at Timoleague (anglicized for Teach Molaga) was built by Donal Glas MacCarthy on the site of an early Celtic Christian church.

IN LOVING MEMORY
OF
JOHN CAL

PAGES 136–137: Detail of a gravestone in the fourteenth century friary at Timoleague, Co. Cork. Like so many Ecclesiastical ruins, Timoleague is now an ancient graveyard.

ABOVE: Blarney Castle, County Cork. Who hasn't heard of the castle and its famous Blarney stone that has the power to give all that kiss it the gift of the gab? With its origins in 1446, the tower in whose machiolations the stone rests is one of the biggest in Ireland.

RIGHT: St. Colman's cathedral looms above Cobh as fishing boats rest along the quays in Cobh Harbor. Cobh prospered during the Victorian era, during which it was known as Queenstown following a visit by the British monarch.

BELOW: Cork City is nestled along the River Lee, its centre situated on an island, bordered by the North and South channels. Cork, anglicized from the Irish *Corcaigh*, is a word that loosely translates to marsh.

LEFT: Looking across the south entrance of Baltimore Harbour, County Cork, from the Beacon to Sherkin Island. *David Lyons*

RIGHT: View from Sherkin Island, looking northeast over Ordree Point toward Baltimore and the Beacon. *David Lyons*

PAGES 144–145: Among the most idyllic places in West Cork is the bucolic park at Guagan Barra.

LEFT: A view east in the afternoon finds road traffic negotiating the confines of the main street at Schull, Co. Cork.

PAGES 148–149, TOP: Morning view of Schull Harbor, Co. Cork. The ferry from Schull to Clear runs at regular times.

PAGES 148–149, BELOW LEFT: A bright afternoon Irish Rail station at Mallow, Co. Cork. Mallow enjoys a good railway service as it is the junction for Dublin-Cork and Dublin-Kerry routes. "Change at Mallow" is a phrase familiar to Irish-rail passengers.

PAGES 148–149, BELOW RIGHT: Foreboding rocky landscape of Mizen Head, Co. Cork on a foggy morning.

ABOVE LEFT: The *Gateway Bar* Cork.

LEFT The megalithic Shronebirrane stone circle lies in a remote, isolated valley on the Kerry side of the Beara Peninsula,

ABOVE: The serene Glanmore Lake reflects hues of an evening sky. Off the beaten path, the Glanmore Valley is only reachable by a dead-end road near the boarder between Kerry and Cork on the Beara Peninsula.

BELOW: The ringed Leacanabuaile stone fort is a few miles northwest of Cahirciveen, Co. Kerry. Although the stones have survived the ages, other portions of this ancient structure decayed centuries ago.

LEFT: At Tralee, Kerry's largest town, a stone church steeple rises above a town park on the town's southwest side.

BELOW: Looking south toward Blennerville provides a view of the Slieve Mish Mountains on the Dingle Peninsula.

PAGES 156–157: Although surrounded by natural scenic splendor, residents of Tralee often prefer the convenience of their own town parks.

BELOW: Kerry's Iveragh Peninsula includes Valencia Island located off the western coast near Cahirciveen. The rugged landscape offers many grand vistas of the island and Dingle Bay beyond.

LEFT: Ogham stones used a simple script consisting of patterned line sequences to convey basic messages, often regarding property ownership or of human burial. Most common in southwest Ireland, these Ogham stones are located in a field on the Dingle Peninsula.

ABOVE: The old Tralee & Dingle Railway was a steeply graded narrow gauge line connecting its namesake towns. Closed because of hard times in the 1950s, portions of the old line are still evident,

including this ruined viaduct at Lispole on Dingle Peninsula.

PAGES 162–163: The Gaelic revival produced renewed interest in early Celtic Christian designs. These Celtic Crosses at a graveyard in Killarney emulate the style of Celtic High crosses from the ninth and tenth centuries. Killarney's Lough Leane is in distance.

PAGES 164–165: The bucolic splendor of Killarney National Park has attracted visitors for centuries. This twilight silhouette of Lough Leane shows the Tomies and Purple Mountains in the distance.

BELOW: The Dingle Peninsula's Minard Castle was a stronghold of the famed Knights of Kerry. Wrecked by Cromwell's armies around 1650, it is now shelter for sheep and wildlife.

BELOW: Stone wall and abandoned farm house dot the side of a hill at Slea Head overlooking Dingle Bay. A tree-less wind swept landscape, the bluish hills of the Iveragh Peninsula can be seen across Dingle Bay.

ABOVE: Faran Beehive Huts at Slea Head above Dingle Bay. These austere dwellings were probably used by monks.

RIGHT: View from inside Faran Beehive Hut looking out at Slea Head above Dingle Bay—Bá an Daingin.

LEFT: The changeable weather on the Dingle
Peninsula can present four seasons in just a few
hours. A momentary flash of winter sun
illuminates houses along a winding road on Slea
Head, Dingle Peninsula.

ABOVE: Mist crawls over the rocky landscape of the
Conor Pass on Dingle Peninsula.

BELOW: A ruined house at Slea Head overlooks Blasket Sound. The legacy of the nineteenth century Diaspora are numerous vacant homes across rural Ireland.

PAGES 182–183 AND ABOVE: Two views of the
Blasket Islands, off the Dingle peninsula. The aerial
view (PAGES 182–183) shows the ruins of a village
on Great Blasket (the island is uninhabited today)
with An Tráigh Bhán beach at top. ABOVE Inish
Tearaght—the most westerly island. *David Lyons*

184

ABOVE: Dursey Island, County Cork. With its monastery ruin, crop ridges, deserted villages, and Oiléan Beag promontory fort, it is one of the quietist places in the county. Dursey today has few inhabitants, no pubs, and no shops. It does, however, boast a cable-car service connecting the island to the mainland and unrivaled birdspotting.
David Lyons

BELOW: The Fahan beehive huts have a panoramic view of Dingle Bay and the Iveragh Peninsula beyond. Simple stone construction has allowed these dwellings to survive for centuries.

PAGES 188–189: Exceptional age and a distinctively contoured roof makes the stone Gallarus Oratory a memorable feature of the Dingle Peninsula.

BELOW: Rural roads, lush landscapes, and minimal modern intrusion make the Dingle Peninsula a throwback to a simpler time.

BELOW: Looking back over the Upper Lake in the Killarney National Park, beyond are Muckross Lake, Lough Leane, and Killarney town.

PAGES 196–197: Skellig Michael showing the two lighthouses and monastery site on right-hand pinnacle. Originally, two lighthouses were established in 1826; the upper was discontinued as early as 1870. The other, on Skellig Michael's southwestern extremity, was completely rebuilt and reestablished in May 1967. It was subsequently made automatic in 1987.

THE WEST OF IRELAND
CLARE, GALWAY, MAYO AND SLIGO

BELOW: A view across fields, bluffs and islands off the coast of Galway northwest of Clifden.

THE WEST OF IRELAND
CLARE, GALWAY, MAYO AND SLIGO

Today's visitors may be awed by Clare, but this has not always been true; centuries ago Clare was viewed as a hard, raw and difficult place to eke out a living. Its attractions include some of Ireland's most impressive geology. With a vertical rise some 650 feet above the North Atlantic, the jagged shale and sandstone littoral known as Cliffs of Moher present a breathtaking sight. The scale of these cliffs are difficult to grasp. Spotting the tiny specks that are sea birds flying hundreds of feet below helps put the magnitude of the cliffs in a human perspective. The cliffs are rightfully one of Ireland's most visited attractions. However, equally as impressive, but rarely visited, is the long peninsula that terminates in a point at Loop Head. Home to a lighthouse and many seabirds, if any place could be described at the "end of the earth" this is it. Standing at the far edge of Loop Head, with waves crashing against the cliffs below and the Atlantic all around, you can look back up the Clare coast where the rising cliffs seem to go on to infinity.

Among Clare's most unusual features is the exposed limestone region known as the Burren. This is a landscape out of dreams—or nightmares. Extending for many miles, fissured blue-gray limestone makes up the ground. While it may appear barren, in fact, the Burren is rich with life. A variety of plants thrive in the cracked limestone including a host of wild flowers and mosses.

Clare is host to many interesting towns and villages. Doolin—Irish *Dú Linn* may be translated as Black Pool, which has the same meaning as *Dubh Linn*, 'Dublin'—is an ocean side village in the virtual shadow of the Cliffs of Moher, that has been developed as cultural hot spot for

traditional Irish Music. Miltown Malbay, near the rocky hazardous bay of Spanish Point, is another lovely town well known for its brightly colored buildings.

Another of Ireland's most famous railway lines, the narrow gauge West Clare Railway, once connected Ennis, Ennistymon, Miltown Malbay, Kilkee, and Kilrush. Although the towns along the line were desperately poor, the scenery characterized by bog, and the service infrequent, the old West Clare attracted a great following, in part because of the famous song by Percy French called *Are ye Right There, Michael,* but also because of its charming, quaint operation resonated with visitors. Even 50 years ago the line harked back to a simpler time. The West Clare was about traveling, not about getting there—since the railway was never very fast, and details such as arrival was occasionally in doubt anyway. The line was closed in 1961. In recent years a short section of line at Moyasta has been rebuilt and is open seasonally for short excursions.

With so much stone on offer, and so few trees, County Clare has its share of man made rock piles in the form of prehistoric antiquities, ecclesiastical sites, and castles. The Poulnabrone Dolman on the Burren is probably the most recognizable of all Ireland's hundreds of megalithic tombs. The shape and dimensions of this stone edifice has captured great interest over the years. Dysert O'Dea is the location of another significant monastic site and a stone tower house castle. The Irish name *Díseart* has Latin origins, and infers a place "deserted". Located in a grassy glen south of Corrofin, Dysert O'Dea embodies a forlorn beauty common to many ecclesiastical Irish ruins. Presumably it was the bucolic splendor of such places that originally attracted people to establish them as spiritual centers, but as such places gradually evolved as power centers, inevitable power struggles occurred leading to violence and destruction. Dysert O'Dea was the site of several significant conflicts over the centuries. Near here, the O'Brien clan made their fourteenth century stand against Anglo-Norman invaders, led by Sir Richard de Clare, and won. It was a different tale altogether when Cromwell's armies arrived in the seventeenth century. A medieval High Cross survives near the ruins of the church and round tower.

Galway is another county of contrasts. Galway city has

BELOW: Among the best known places in Clare is the ocean-side village of Doolin.

ABOVE: Moss covered vestiges of a pre-historic ring fort, or "*cathair*" in the Burren, Co. Clare. Thousands of these remnants of early settlement dot the Irish countryside. Many are marked on Ordinance Survey maps.

RIGHT: Ireland's Cliffs of Moher is a vision of sheer verticality. This view looks south toward Hags Head, the Victorian O'Brien castle perched on a ledge gives a sense of scale.

BELOW: Rough seas are slowly eroding the coast of Clare, even the massive Cliffs of Moher in the distance are not immune to the force of the North Atlantic.

BELOW: Cracked limestone slabs characteristic of the Burren line the beach near the Cliffs of Moher.

RIGHT: A strange sight harking back to early civilized man; the Poulnabrone portal dolman rests on the cracked limestone of the Burren, Co. Clare.

INSET: The Poulnabrone portal dolman in the Burren dates to at least 2,000 BC and is among the most famous stone age ruins in the west of Ireland.

BELOW: The rocky plateau known as The Burren—anglicized from the Irish *Boireann*—appears as barren limestone, however in reality it is host to a great variety of plant life, including many rare flowers that flourish between cracks in the stone.

ABOVE LEFT: The village of Clifden, Co. Galway was developed in the early nineteenth century. It sits in view of the towering Twelve Bens mountains.

BELOW LEFT: Dusk along the Connemara coast finds a ruined farm house against a stormy sky. Depopulation of rural Ireland in the nineteenth century left many ruined houses.

ABOVE: This castle near Clifden was built about 1815 by John D'Arcy, Sheriff of Galway and founder of Clifden town.

RIGHT: What better home could a romantic poet have than a fourteenth century rural Galway tower house? Ireland's premier poet W.B. Yeats purchased Thoor Bally, restored it and lived there for around a decade. Today it's a museum.

PAGES 226–227: Clifden Harbor is just a short distance down from the town which is built on bluff above the bay.

BELOW: A small boat called "Coleraine", rests in the quayside at Clifden, the town is on the bluff beyond.

RIGHT: A stone gate left over from the fourteenth century town wall survives at Athenry, Co. Galway. The name of the town in Irish is *Átha an Rí* meaning "ford of the kings".

ABOVE LEFT: Visions from the Celtic legend, Children of Lir: Swans swim in a rocky estuary along the Connemara coast.

BELOW LEFT: There are more sheep in Ireland than people. Here a lone ewe wanders the Connemara under overcast skies.

ABOVE: The west of Ireland is known for its ever damp weather. A magenta evening sky reaches down to the ground on the Connemara Coast.

BELOW: This rural road near Athenry, Co. Galway features blossoming trees on a spring evening.

BELOW: Evening light in November reveals arrow slits in the Norman castle wall at Athenry which tell of anticipated violent times long ago. The town was sacked by Hugh Roe O'Donnell at the end of the sixteenth century.

PAGES 234–235: The Dominican Priory at Athenry was established in 1241, although these ruins are largely from the fifteenth century.

LEFT: Athenry is an Anglicization of the Irish name *Baile Átha an Rí* —*Baile* is Irish for "town", *Átha* for "ford", and *Rí* for "king".

BELOW: Although intact, the round tower at Kilmacduagh leans out from the center. Kilmacduagh is a few miles from the market town of Gort, Co. Galway.

PREVIOUS PAGE: Derryclare Lough, ten miles east of Clifden, in Connemara.

LEFT: Galway has a flare for festivals and pageantry making it a popular attraction year round.

BELOW: Once Galway's town common, the lush environs of Eyre Square is now the city's largest public park. At the west side are the bus and railway terminals and the old Great Southern Hotel—once owned by the railway company, and now the Hotel Meyrick.

PAGES 242–243: Dun Aenghus ancient stone fort high on the cliffs of Inishmore, Aran Islands, County Galway. One of the most magnificently sited ancient monuments in Europe, it sits atop 200ft sheer cliffs, at least half its structure now eroded by the sea. *David Lyons*

BELOW: On May 10, 2003, a Railway Preservation Society of Ireland excursion train rolls toward Westport on the annual "Two-Day tour" over Iarnród Éireann (Irish Rail). Mayo's famous Croagh Patrick looms large in the distance.

BELOW: A classic humpback three-arch stone bridge carries a street over Carrowbeg River in Westport.

BELOW: Georgian splendor Mayo style, Westport was laid out in the 1770s. The arch bridge carries a street over the channeled Carrowbeg River.

BELOW: A rural Mayo farm yard wall with an old bell tower.

BELOW: Westport's Octagon in blue glow of early evening. At the center of the square is a Statue of Westport benefactor George Glendenning.

BELOW: Fishing boat at sunset at Westport quay in evening light. At one time Westport Harbor saw considerable commerce; it imported coal, corn, and salt, while exporting agricultural produce and timber.

BOTTOM: Looking south on the main street in Foxford: the Church of Ireland is lit up on the left, while shops and pubs are on the right. Proximity to the River Moy and several large fresh water lakes has made Foxford popular with anglers.

PAGES 254–255: Churchyard with Celtic crosses silhouette and a dark sky. Based on the medieval Christian High Crosses, Celtic crosses have become a form of grave marker.

BELOW: Located at the limit of navigation on the Moy estuary, Ballina, Co. Mayo has developed as one of the region's important market towns.

258

LEFT: In Sligo town, swans grace the river known in Irish as *Sligeach*.

ABOVE: This is W.B. Yeats' country; County Sligo as viewed from the foot of Ben Bulbin.

BELOW: William Butler Yeats (1865-1939) is Ireland's most famous poet. He is often associated with this area of Sligo about which he wrote. He is buried in the graveyard at Drumcliff.

BELOW: The *Sligeach* or River Garavogue flows from Lough Gill to Sligo Bay through Sligo town. A sizable market town and a modest sized port, Sligo is among the more important large towns in the west of Ireland.

BELOW: Seen at sunset, this larg[...]
Carrowmore makes for a pictu[...]
among lush green fields.

BELOW: Rising 1,725 feet above sea level, Ben
Bulbin resembles a verdant mesa. The Irish *Binn
Ghulbain* infers Beak Pinnacle which describes, as
much as names this unusual mountain.

BELOW: The megalithic burial[...]
Carrowmore is the resting pla[...]
remains nearly 7,000 years ol[...]
the stones at Carrowmore ma[...]
through their relative positio[...]

BELOW: Ben Bulbin is just a few miles north of Sligo town.

ULSTER
DONEGAL AND NORTHERN IRELAND

BELOW: Fresh water feeds a tidal pool on the shores
of Malin Head in the light of a spring evening.

ULSTER
DONEGAL AND NORTHERN IRELAND

Ulster is one of four traditional Irish provinces, the other three being Connacht, Leinster, and Munster. Ulster consists of the nine counties of the north, six of which are now administered as Northern Ireland and have remained part of the United Kingdom. These are Antrim, Armagh, Derry, Down, Fermanagh, and Tyrone. The remaining three counties—Cavan, Donegal, and Monaghan—are part of the Irish Republic. For many years the border between Northern Ireland and the Republic was manned with customs and check points, but times have changed and border controls have been lifted, allowing people to pass freely between the northern counties and those in the Republic. Today, one may cross county lines without even realizing it. Superficial differences are subtle;

in Northern Ireland phone boxes are operated by British Telecom rather than Eircom, and the post office is the Royal Mail with its red post boxes, rather than An Post with its green boxes. The politics of the North are another story, and sadly the region's "Troubles" through the 1990s were news everywhere. Since the Good Friday Agreement of 1998, the situation has largely calmed.

Belfast is the largest city in Northern Ireland. It was one of the most industrialized portions of Ireland, famous for its shipyards and harbor. While the city has a number of fine old buildings, it lacks the cohesive Georgian charm of Dublin and, like many cities across the Irish Sea, it has suffered from urban renewal and the cutting of modern motorways though parts of the city center. In recent years

the waterfront has been cleaned up and considerable new construction is changing the face of the city.

Derry—or Londonderry—is the region's second largest population center. This picturesque town set along the River Foyle has its origins in an early Christian monastery, but is known for its long and troubled history. It was the site of several long sieges in the seventeenth century when its famous walls withstood the forces trying to penetrate them. Derry's city walls have survived the test of time and are among the most intact medieval walls in Europe. Sadly, in the 1960s and 1970s Derry became notorious for its role in the Northern Irish "Troubles". Its most famous incident was on January 30, 1972, when British troops fired upon civilians in a civil rights march killing 14 people, an event known ever after as Bloody Sunday and remembered by a popular U2 song from the 1980s. Derry is a visually fascinating place made more interesting by its history.

Ulster is blessed with some of Ireland's most beautiful and most dramatic scenery and some of its most interesting archeological features. The rugged Antrim coast is famous for its tall cliffs, rocky promenades, and most of all the unusual geological feature known as the Giant's Causeway. In Irish this is *Cloghán-na-bhFomhraigh,* "the stepping stones of the Fomorians". Celtic legends tell of earlier races of giants, among them the Fomorians, that inhabited Ireland in ancient times. Legends aside, the Causeway owes its creation to events more than 60 million years ago when lava flows crystallized to form basalt columns with a polygonical profile. Years of erosion have exposed these columns which extend from the cliff sides into the North Atlantic. Most of the columns are hexagonal shaped. They have been a popular attraction since the eighteenth century when they were classified by some scholars as among of the natural wonders of the world. The towering cliffs around the Giant's Causeway add to the other-worldliness of the setting.

A few miles further west along the coast is Dunluce Castle, famous for its precarious location and its tragic history. The original fourteenth century castle on this site is understood to have been built by the Earl of Ulster. Much

BELOW: On Donegal's Horn Head traffic isn't an issue. This narrow road leads toward Dunfanaghy.

of the surviving structure on the promontory dates from the late mid-sixteenth century when it was the stronghold of the MacDonnells who ruled northern Ulster. The castle is remembered for the night of an ill-fated banquet on a stormy evening in 1639, when the kitchen was battered by winds, collapsed and fell in to the ocean taking with it several servants. The story goes that afterward, the lady of the house refused to set foot in the castle and new buildings were constructed on the cliffs south of the promontory. Ultimately the family relocated altogether, and today the castle is one of Ulster's most famous ruins.

County Fermanagh is a contrast to Antrim. Where Antrim is famous for its coast, Fermanagh is known for its lakes and forests that give it an especially bucolic quality. The Lough Erne water network is the county's most prominent feature. Enniskillen straddles an island in the River Erne which flows between upper and lower lakes. Here a classic castle sits against the backdrop of the town making for a storybook setting. On the south side of lower Lough Erne is the ruin of Tully Castle, now surrounded by beautiful manicured gardens. Among the strangest and most fascinating antiquities are the pagan or early Christian statues at the Caldragh Graveyard on Boa Island on the north side of the lake. These were carved by unknown artists some 1,500 years ago. Other ancient statues are built into a wall located on White Island and may be as old as the seventh century.

County Donegal remains one of Ireland's most remote and most rural places. It has no cities, and its largest town, Letterkenny, is not very big. Donegal is known for scenic splendor, but not its good weather. Often battered by storms, its been known to rain in Donegal for days without end. Malin Head at the top of the Inishowen Peninsula is Ireland's most northerly point and, as Donegal is part of the Republic, it is notably further north than any point in Northern Ireland. Working west along the Donegal coast are a series of peninsulas that reach into the Atlantic. Fanad Head is separated from Inishowen by Lough Swilly, which despite its name is an estuary of the Atlantic and not a freshwater lake. Beyond is Melmore Head, and Rinnafaghla Point, and across the body of water known in Irish as *Cuan na gCaorach,* "Sheep Haven", is the Horn Head, which, like much of Donegal has a significantly larger population of sheep than of humans. This rocky, windswept point offers spectacular views of the distant Mucklish and Derry Veagh Mountains to the south, and the endless expanse of the Atlantic to the North and West. The view is lost on the resident sheep which are more interested in chewing the grass in front of them than pondering the great beyond. Every so often, an unfortunate sheep strays to close to a cliff-side and falls in the unforgiving ocean below.

Donegal is one of several Irish counties no longer served

by rail. At one time the county was blessed with a number of quaint narrow gauge lines that traversed some of the best scenery of any railway on the island. These were, however, abandoned in the 1950s although a short section of railway line at Fintown has been reopened and now operates with a vintage railcar of the kind once used here decades ago. This seasonal attraction combines authentic railway equipment

with the thrill of a splendid scenic ride along Lough Finn.

Donegal's most dramatic natural feature is Slieve League on its southwest peninsula, beyond Donegal town, and the fishing village of Killybegs. Here, the mountain rises 595 meters out of Donegal Bay. Substantially taller than the Cliffs of Moher in Clare, Slieve League does not present the sheer drop of the more famous cliffs.

BELOW: Looking downhill on the main street of Letterkenny, Donegal's most important town, which is well accommodated by ample numbers of pubs.

BELOW: Looking across placid waters at the village of Dunfanaghy, Co. Donegal toward Horn Head.

LEFT: Sunset off the coast near Dunfanaghy reveals the length of Tory Island. Ferry's connect Tory Island with Magheroarty and Bunbeg, yet it remains one of Ireland's most remote places. The legendary Fomorian giants are said to have come from there.

ABOVE: On the promenade at Horn Head, Co. Donegal, a lone sheep contemplates the vast ocean beyond, or perhaps the tasty patch of grass between where it stands and the edge of the cliff.

BELOW: Donegal coast as seen from Malin Head.

ABOVE LEFT: Interior of the restored Jacobean style Manor House adjacent to Donegal Castle, in Donegal town.

BELOW LEFT: Home to Red Hugh O'Donnell in the sixteenth century, the ruins of Donegal Castle can be seen along the bank of the River Eske in Donegal town. O'Donnell famously escaped from Dublin Castle to lead an ill-fated rebellion.

ABOVE: Detail of the ruins of Donegal Castle show the apex of a stone arch doorway. The roof was burned centuries ago.

BELOW: Fireplace inside and storage area convey the spirit of an earlier era at Donegal Castle, Donegal town.

BELOW: Remains of a stone fortress on a
promenade at Carrigan Head near Slieve League,
Co. Donegal.

BELOW: The cliffs at Slieve League are some of the tallest in Europe, and while less vertical than the Cliffs of Moher are substantially higher.

BELOW: Rural byway—the road to Malin Head wanders up into a fog.

RIGHT: The Fleet Inn along the main street in Kilcar, Co. Donegal on a raw, damp summer's morning. How do you know Summer in Donegal? The daylight lasts longer.

ABOVE: Detail of Celtic Cross with traditional pattern at Donegal town.

RIGHT: Rays of the setting sun trace the clouded sky at Malin Head.

BELOW: Located on a broad hill top near Raphoe, Co. Donegal is the Beltony stone circle. Consisting of 60 stones, one set apart from the others, this spectacular bronze age monument takes its name from the pagan May Day celebration, Beltane.

PREVIOUS PAGE: Harry Avery's
Castle in County Tyrone is a
good example of medieval
military architecture.
Associated with the O'Neill's,
the story goes that Aimhréidh
O'Neill had a sister with the
head of a pig. The castle was
offered as dowry—but all the
suitors who refused her after
seeing her would be hanged.
It is said that 19 men
preferred this fate! *David
Lyons*

LEFT: View west across White
Rocks Beach to Portrush,
County Antrim. *David Lyons*

BELOW: In recent times Derry was famous for its role in the "Troubles". Its graphic murals have attracted world wide attention. Perhaps even more famous is the U2 song *Sunday Bloody Sunday* inspired by the tragic events of January 30, 1972.

YOU ARE NOW ENTERING FREE DERRY

BELOW: Pastoral splendor near Bolea, Co. Derry. Sheep graze contentedly on a blustery March afternoon. In the distance Keady Mountain rises above Springwell Forest.

BELOW: The town of Portballintrae is on the Antrim coast near the Giant's Causeway. This day 100 mph winds and rough seas were battering the coast, despite sunny weather.

BELOW: The scenic splendor of the rugged Antrim coast as viewed from the ruins of Dunluce Castle.

BELOW INSET: The view along the north Antrim coast toward Portrush from Dunluce Castle. During a banquet in 1639, the kitchen of the castle was torn by winds and plunged into the sea along with servants preparing the dinner.

BELOW: The strange geometric basalt columns of the Giant's Causeway were formed an estimated 60-61 million years ago from cooling lava flows. Today it is easy to step from stone to stone bringing one dangerously close to the fury of the North Atlantic.

PAGES 316–317: The spectral ruins and vista of the sea make Dunluce Castle a hauntingly beautiful place.

LEFT: In the deep and narrow confines of the Sloughran Glen, Co. Tyrone is the unusual confluence of streams caused by adjacent waterfalls.

BELOW LEFT: Twin waterfalls in the Sloughran Glen allow for perpetual mist that enables verdant mosses to grow on the trees and walls of the chasm.

RIGHT: One of two waterfalls cascading over the rocks at Sloughran Glen, Co. Tyrone.

BELOW: A church basks in the sun on a May morning near Poyntz Pass, Co. Armagh.

BELOW: Belturbit, Co. Cavan is an awkward situated town on a hillside along the main Dublin—Cavan—Enniskillen Road near the shores of Upper Lough Erne.

ABOVE: Displayed at Belfast's Donegall Quay along the west bank of the River Lagan is this a thirty-two foot long ceramic Salmon by Northern Irish artist John Kindness.

LEFT: Sun glistens on the black waters of Lower Lough Erne, County Fermanagh. The pastoral and bucolic lakes of rural Fermanagh comprises some the most pleasant inland scenery in Ireland.

ABOVE: The Caldragh Graveyard on Boa Island in Lower Lough Erne, County Fermanagh is home to a pair of early Celtic Pagan/Christian statues. The more significant of the two is a Janus figure depicting a man and a woman back to back.

RIGHT: Constructed between 1612 and 1615, the famed Tully Castle in Co. Fermanagh was the scene of a brutal massacre during the wars of 1641. In recent years the property has been repaired and cleaned up and since 1988 has been decorated with gardens.

BELOW: Enniskillen, Co. Fermanagh has a fairytale look about it. Its castle and churches are situated along the water connecting Upper and Lower Lough Erne. Once a strategic fortress, the castle is now a museum.

THE MIDLANDS
KILDARE, TIPPERARY, OFFALY, LAOIS AND KILKENNY

BELOW: This boreen at Cappagh, Co. Tipperary leading toward the Galty Mountains is not found on many maps.

THE MIDLANDS
KILDARE, TIPPERARY, OFFALY, LAOIS AND KILKENNY

Unlike coastal or mountainous counties, the Irish Midlands are not known for captivating scenery and have been too often overlooked because of their relative blandness. Yet, in many ways, the Midlands represents the real Ireland, an honest place unfettered by notions of itself. True, the scenery is not dramatic and its big towns are not special as they tend to be crowded and lined with moderately old, but uninspiring buildings, but the Midlands have plenty more subtle attractions. There are many lovely smaller towns and villages where people are friendly, pace of life is relaxed, and traffic jams are more likely to be caused by an elderly farmer herding his sheep down the main road than by excessive automobiles.

Ireland's two major canal networks were forged across the Midlands in the latter part of the eighteenth century. Both connected Dublin with the Shannon, thus allowing for a trans-Irish transport system. The Grand Canal was built first and takes a southerly route via Sallins, Co. Kildare, and Tullamore, Co. Offaly, joining the River Shannon at Shannon Harbor, a few miles up river from Banagher, Co Offaly. Several branches of the canal were built, including one that angled southward via Monasterevin to Athy, Co. Kildare where the canal ties in with the River Barrow. The Royal Canal was started and completed a generation later, and runs west from Dublin by way of Maynooth, Enfield and Mullingar. In today's highway-minded world, where we take the ability to cover 10 miles in 10 minutes by car racing down the motorway for granted, it is difficult to grasp the

transport revolution that occurred when the canals opened up the Irish Midlands in Georgian times. Towns along the canals flourished as a result of improved transportation. Likewise a variety of businesses prospered as a result of being able to efficiently ship their products. Among the commodities moved by canal were bricks, coal, grain, limestone, and stout. Guinness's St. James's Gate Brewery was adjacent to the original main terminal of the Grand Canal at St. James Street Harbor, and the combination of a superior product with improved transport gave Guinness an edge over its competition. The Royal Canal was never as extensive or as useful as the Grand Canal. Its water level route proved desirable for the Midland Great Western Railway which acquired the Royal Canal in the 1850s, and built its line parallel to the canal as far as Mullingar. When railways opened they killed the canals' passenger business, yet the canals continued to offer low cost freight transport for another century. The Royal Canal was closed to traffic first, while the Grand Canal carried its last freight in 1960, which consisted of Guinness kegs. Following years of disuse,

portions of the old canals have been redeveloped for pleasure craft and again offer an easy paced way to enjoy the Midland countryside. A number of the old canal side pubs that thrived because of their easy access to stout are still open. And while old-timers have complained that the stout hasn't tasted the same since Guinness stopped shipping by canal, its still possible to enjoy a canal-side pint.

Located in fields right off the present main Dublin to Waterford road (soon to be supplanted by a modern motorway), Jerpoint Abbey south of Thomastown, Co. Kilkenny, is an excellent example of a former Cistercian monastery. The origins of the abbey are not exactly clear, but it was founded in the twelfth century, expanded in the thirteenth century and flourished for nearly 350 years. Like most Irish monastic institutions, it was suppressed by King Henry VIII's dissolution. Of special interest are the ornate carvings in the walls of the cloister.

Located in a small rural graveyard in south County Tipperary a few miles north of Carrick-on-Suir are the famed Ahenny High Crosses, which are considered some of

the best examples of this variety of characteristic Irish ecclesiastical art. Co. Tipperary is better known for the "Rock of Cashel", a prominently situated monastic site and castle above the town of Cashel. (The Irish *Caiseal* translates as "stone fort".) A church had existed on this site since at least the seventh century. It became known as the seat of power to Ireland's powerful eleventh century leader Brian Boru and, while the players changed with the times, the Rock remained a place of political power until the fifteenth century. As with the case of many of Ireland's walled towns and other prominent monastic institutions, it was ruined by assaults from Cromwell's armies in the mid-seventeenth century. For many years the Rock was a main feature for travelers on the main Dublin-Cork road, but the opening of the Cashel bypass a few years ago now directs most traffic away from the town.

Several miles north of Cashel is the Holycross Abbey, located near Thurles. For Irish sport enthusiasts, the town of Thurles has special significance: in 1884, the Gaelic Athletic Association was founded here at the Hayes Hotel. The Hotel is still on the town's main square and features a classic daytime carvery with ample portions to satisfy most appetites.

Along the River Shannon at Clonmacnoise, Co. Offaly, is a well known monastery with High Crosses, and ruined castle. The monastery was founded in the sixth century and developed as one Ireland's most significant Christian sites, famous for the early Irish text *Lebor na hUidre,* "book of the Dún Cow". Consistent with other significant monastic sites, Clonmacnoise is beautifully and prominently situated. However its easy access to Shannon resulted in repeated sackings over the centuries. It was thoroughly wrecked in the sixteenth century. The visitor's center at Clonmacnoise is well prepared for visits from the faithful who come from far and wide to inspect the ruins.

PAGES 330–331: A rainbow graces the winter sky over the Railway Bar at Clonmel, Co. Tipperary. *Cluain Meala* can be translated as "Meadow of Honey". Today, as the home to Bulmers Cider, Clonmel is better known for its apples.

RIGHT: Grave stones and Celtic Crosses at the Rock of Cashel looking northward.

PAGES 334–335: Detailed carving in the stone ruins at Cashel.

BELOW: A steam tractor rally at Stradbally, Co. Laois insures a good bit of excitement and delightful shrill whistles.

PAGES 354–355: Clear evening in a quiet village: the lights of the Signal Box Pub at Ballybrophy, Co. Laois entices the infrequent passer-by. Sadly, this quaint trackside pub has since closed, its lights beckon no more.

NORTH OF DUBLIN

BELOW: The British Admiralty requirement of 90-feet of clearance over the mouth of the Boyne led to construction of one of Ireland's most impressive nineteenth century bridges: Great Northern Railway's Boyne Viaduct, at Drogheda, Co. Louth.

NORTH OF DUBLIN

The Valley of Boyne has great significance for Ireland. A detailed study of its sights, sites, and ruins can present no better Irish history lesson. The passage tombs at Newgrange, Knowth, and Dowth are some of the oldest evidence of advanced intelligent civilization on the island. These are situated on the north side of the Boyne Valley. The people who erected these timeless monuments are entirely a mystery. The stones were already considered ancient when Celtic peoples began to settle in Ireland in the second millennia BC, and Irish legends evolved with references to the people who came from the time before. Where Celtic legends provide colorful stories, and modern theories offer conjectural explanations, yet no one really knows why these relics were built, but it's obvious that the

great skill and effort was involved with their construction. The exceptional longevity of these sites continues to awe all who gaze upon them. Further up the valley is the Hill of Tara, long deemed one of Europe's most significant prehistoric sites. Shrouded in layers of myth, Tara has resonated with power since the stone age. It is said to have been home to Ireland's legendary seductress Queen Madb. Tara has been burial ground for at least 5,500 years. It was a site of pagan significance and became a powerbase for Ireland's high kings Not far away on the opposite side of the valley the Hill of Slane is where St. Patrick is lit his Pascal Fire. This site emerged as significant monastic institution early in Christian Ireland.

The importance of the Boyne as an avenue of commerce

RIGHT: Located along the Boyne, Slane, Co. Meath has a long and fascinating history. Atop the hill are the ruins of Slane Abbey built in 1512. More than a thousand years earlier, St. Patrick lit the Pascal fire here to celebrate Easter

BELOW: Close-up of the St. Patrick statue at the ruins of Slane Abbey.

BELOW: The gravestones at Slane Abbey are seen against the bucolic splendor of Meath farmland in the Boyne Valley.

RIGHT: Although an ancient monastic site since the time of St. Patrick, the ruins atop the hill of Slane are largely those of the abbey built in 1512, more than a millennia after Patrick had stood here.

ABOVE: Skull and crossbones decorate a grave stone at Slane Abbey.

RIGHT: The Royal Canal catches the evening sky near Enfield, Co. Meath. The Midland Great Western Railway built along the Royal Canal in the 1850s reducing the waterway to a secondary status.

LEFT: Among Ireland's most famous places is Tara, Co. Meath. The motorway scheduled for the area has caused a bit of stir.

BELOW: Ruins in the fog at Navin, Co. Meath

PAGES 376–377: The passage tomb at Newgrange is Ireland's most intriguing prehistoric site. Ancient engineers skillfully arranged the mouth of the tomb so when the sun crests the hill side on the Winter Solstice, the interior space is bathed in light.

ABOVE: The complex swirled patterns carved into Newgrange's entrance stone have become emblematic of Ireland's megalithic heritage.

RIGHT: A ruined wall looms above the trees at Trim. An early seat of Norman power in Ireland, fortifications at Trim guarded a strategic ford of the River Boyne.

FAR RIGHT: This medieval tower at Duleek Church was built adjacent to a much earlier round tower that was subsequentially destroyed. In one sense 'Duleek Church' is redundant, since Duleek has been derived from *'Damhliag'* an old Irish word for Church.

PAGES 388–389: Ruins of Duleek Church bask in the sun on a March afternoon. The medieval tower on the left was constructed in the fifteenth century.

BELOW: The Boyne Valley has been settled by highly intelligent people for at least 5,000 years, as evidence, are numerous relics of early civilization. The valley is also known for its strategic role in political strife in more recent centuries.

PAGES 392–393: The pint and mobile phone are
common accoutrements to patrons of Irish Pubs.
Sean Brown's Hell's Kitchen at Castlerea, Co.
Roscommon, is a popular watering place that
serves an excellent bacon & cabbage dinner.

ABOVE: Trim Castle on the River Boyne, County Meath. One of the great Norman castles of Ireland, Trim was started in the 1170s by the de Laceys and built into the 12th century by the Mortimers. In 1399 two of Richard II's wards, the sons of Bolingbroke, lived there—including Henry of Monmouth, later Henry V.

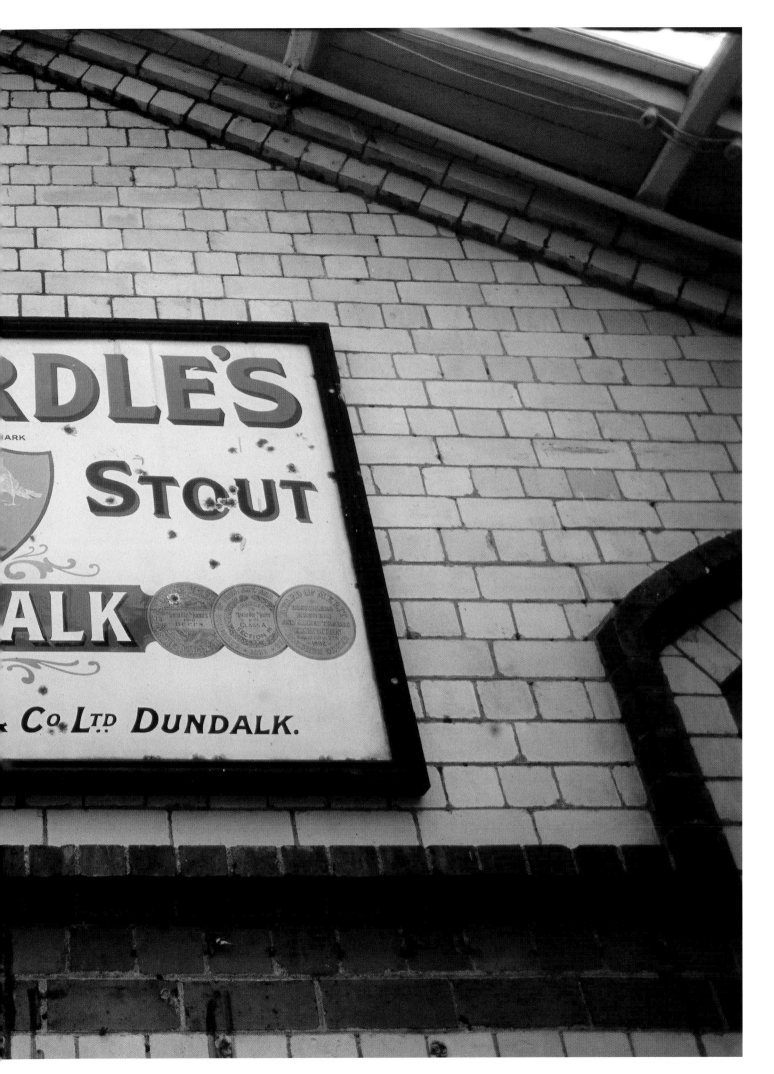

PAGES 396–397: Among the Breweries in Ireland was Macardle's in Dundalk. Formed in 1863, it became part of the Guinness group in 1962. The brewery closed in 2001.

ABOVE: St. Patrick is credited with introducing the Shamrock as a symbol of Christianity. Today it is the most familiar symbol of Ireland.

BIBLIOGRAPHY

Books

— *The Works of W.B. Yeats.* Ware, Hertfordshire: Wordsworth Editions Ltd, 1994.

Behan, Brendan. *After the Wake.* Dublin: The O'Brien Press, 1981.

Bielenberg, Andy. *The Shannon Scheme and the Electrification of the Irish Free State.* Dublin: The Lilliput Press, 2002.

Boland, Gerry. *Stroller's Guide to Dublin.* Dublin: Gill & Macmillan Ltd, 1999.

Bowers, Maira. *Dublin City Parks & Gardens.* Dublin: The Lilliput Press, 1999.

Brady, Joseph and Anngret Simms. *Dublin through Space & Time.* Dublin: Four Courts Press Ltd., 2001, 2002.

Clarke, Peter. *The Royal Canal—the Complete Story.* Dublin: ELO Publication, 1992.

Connolly, James. *The Re-Conquest of Ireland.* Dublin and Belfast: New Books Publications, 1983.

Conroy, J. C. *A History of Railways in Ireland.* London: Longmans, Green and Co. Ltd, 1928.

Corcoran, Michael. *Through Streets Broad & Narrow.* Leicester: Midland Publishing, 2000.

Cox, Ronald and Michael Gould. *Civil Engineering Heritage—Ireland.* London: Thomas Telford Publishing, 1998.

Cox, Ronald and Michael Gould. *Ireland Bridges.* Dublin: Wolfhound Press, 2003.

DeCourcy, J.W. *The Liffey in Dublin.* Dublin: Gill & Macmillan, 1996.

Delvin, Polly. *American Express Travel Guide Dublin.* New York: Prentice Hall, 1993.

Duffy, Seán. *Atlas of Irish History.* Dublin: Gill & Macmillan Ltd, 1997.

Foster, R.E. *Modern Ireland 1600-1972.* London: Penguin Press, 1988.

Flanagan, Deirdre and Laurence Flanagan. *Irish Place Names.* Dublin: Gill & Macmillan, 1994,2002.

Gerard-Sharp, Lisa and Tim Perry. *Eye Witness Travel—Ireland.* London: Dorling Kindersley Ltd., 1995, 2008.

Giedion, Sigfried. *Space, Time and Architecture.* 4th Edition. Cambridge: Harvard University Press, 1963.

Gillespie, Michael Patrick. *The Works of James Joyce.* Ware, Hertfordshire: Wordsworth Editions Ltc, 1995.

Gilligan, Henry A. *A History of the Port of Dublin.* Dublin: Gill & Macmillan Ltd, 1988.

Gray, Paul and Geoff Wallis. *The Rough Guid to Ireland.* New York: Rough Guides, 2006

Jerrares, A. Norman. *Jonathan Swift—The Selected Poems.* London: Kyle Cathie Ltd, 1981.

Johnson, Paul. *Ireland—A Concise History from the Twelfth Century to the Present Day.* Chicago: Academy Chicago Publishers, 1980.

Joyce, P.W. *Irish Local Names Explained.* London: Fitzhouse Books, 1923, 1940.

Judt, Tony. *Postwar—A History of Europe Since 1945.* London: William Heinemann, 2005

Kilfeather, Siobhán. *Dublin—A Cultural History.* Oxford University Press, 2005

Lewis, Samuel. *County Antrim a Topographical Dictionary.* Belfast: Friarbush Press, 2002.

Lawlor, T. Anthony. *Irish Maritime Survey.* Dublin: The Parkside Press Limited, 1945.

Lydon, James. *The Making of Ireland—from Ancient Times to the Present.* London: Routledge, 1998.

Maitiú, Séamas Ó. *Dublin's Suburban Towns 1834-1930.* Dublin: Four Courts Press, 2003.

Manning, Maurice and Moore McDowell. *Electricity Supply in Ireland—The History of the ESB.* Dublin: Gill & Macmillan Ltd, 1984.

Murray, K.A. *Ireland's First Railway.* Dublin: The Irish Railway Record Society, 1981.

O' Farrell, Padraic. *How the Irish Speak English.* Dublin: Mercier Press, 1980, 1993.

Ó Riain, Mícheal. *On the Move—Córas Iompair Éieann 1945-1995.* Dublin: Gill & Macmillan Ltd, 1995.

Ó Siochfhradha. *Foclóir Gaeilge/Béarla — English/Irish.* Dublin: Smurfit Services Ltd. 1996.

Robertson, Ian. *Blue Guide—Ireland.* London: A&C Black, 1987.

Roth, Leland M. *Understanding Architecture: Its Elements, History and Meaning.* Boulder: Westview Press, 1993.

Room, Adrian. *A Dictionary of Irish Place Names.* Belfast: Appletree Press, 1994.

Simmons, Jack. *Rail 150, The Stockton & Darlington Railway and What Followed.* London: Eyre Methuen, 1975.

Solomon, Brian. *Railway Masterpieces, celebrating the world's greatest trains, stations and feats of engineering.* Iola, Wisconsin: Krause, 2002.

Standage, Tom. *A History of the World in 6 Glasses.* New York: Walker Publishing Company, 2006.

Walsh, Claire. *Archaeological Excavation at Patrick, Nicholas & Winetavern Streets Dublin.* Dublin: Brandon, 1997.

Periodicals

Journal of Bridge Engineering. American Society of Civil Engineers, New York.

Journal of the Irish Railway Record Society, Dublin, Ireland.

Proceedings [of the] Blackrock Society, Blackrock, Ireland.

INDEX